For This I Came

For This I Came

*Spiritual wisdom for
priesthood and ministry*

Wyn Beynon

CANTERBURY
PRESS
Norwich

First published in the UK in 2023 by the Canterbury Press Norwich
Editorial office
3rd Floor, Invicta House
108–114 Golden Lane
London EC1Y 0TG, UK
www.canterburypress.co.uk

Canterbury Press is an imprint of Hymns Ancient & Modern Ltd
(a registered charity)

Hymns Ancient & Modern® is a registered trademark of
Hymns Ancient & Modern Ltd
13A Hellesdon Park Road, Norwich
Norfolk NR6 5DR, UK

Gerard Manley Hopkins, 'As Kingfishers Catch Fire', reproduced by
permission of the Licensor Oxford University Press through PLSclear
R. S. Thomas, 'The Priest', *Collected Poems: 1945–1990*, reproduced
by permission of the Licensor Orion Books through PLSclear

British Library Cataloguing in Publication data

A catalogue record for this book is available
from the British Library

978-1-78622-466-8

Typeset by Regent Typesetting
Printed and bound in Great Britain by
CPI Group (UK) Ltd

Contents

For Christ plays in ten thousand places

Lovely in limbs, and lovely in eyes not his

For thine is the kingdom, power and the glory

Now abide: faith, hope and love, these three

Joyful, simple and merciful, according to the gospel

This, here, now

The anatomy of apathy

The marks of a Jesus-shaped mission

Foreword

By the Rt Revd Dr John Inge, Bishop of Worcester

Wyn Beynon's *For This I Came* is a generous book. It is as if Wyn were opening the door of his house and saying, 'Welcome! Come on in. Please enjoy everything you see here. And if something takes your fancy, help yourself, feel free to take it away – it's yours.' Wyn's generosity is all the more extravagant because there are so many gems here to choose from. The free verse – free, there is no charge – is often gnomic: 'The Kingdom is remembering things we never knew we knew.' 'True laughter always includes.' But it is never didactic: Wyn is not trying to tell his reader what to think or believe; rather he is prompting, provoking even, the reader to think for her- or himself and in the process to explore their faith.

The verse may be free, but the structure is intricate. Each titled poem is numbered sequentially. The first are inspired by three poems, by G. M. Hopkins, by R. S. Thomas and one George Herbert: twelve poems for each. Wyn is placing himself and his ministry within the tradition of priests who are poets as well as pastors. The remaining twenty-two have different sources of inspiration, biblical, liturgical, philosophical. All together they cover the whole range of priestly ministry, reflecting on sacraments, identity, mission, power. The structure beautifully conveys the variety and the unity of the ordained life.

And, of course, that life is Wyn's own life. He draws on his forty years of experience and prayer. He is open, honest, intimate. He clearly believes with a passion that the calling of a Christian is to live life undefended because this is how Jesus lived his life, this is the life of resurrection.

The advantage of words over objects is that you can take words away and still leave them there. I hope you will accept Wyn's invitation to help yourself, knowing that countless others can do the same.

Introduction

You have been called. You have been called to be a member of the body of Christ. You are unique and indispensable and yet you carry this treasure in earthen vessels. You have been called to love your neighbour as yourself. You have been called to be the child and servant of God.

It may be that you have also felt the call to ordination, to priesthood, and are exploring what on earth that could mean. It may be that you answered the call long ago, or are preparing for ordination, or are newly ordained. You are not a youth worker or an evangelist, not a worship leader or a manager, not at pastor or a soul friend, or a preacher. All those are hugely important tasks. Thank God for those who faithfully minister in those ways.

But *you* have been called to be a priest. At times priesthood will include some, but not too many, of those other tasks.

I offer you this little book about priesthood to encourage you and to try and nudge you away from being distracted by so many necessary tasks. Priesthood, if faithfully and selflessly followed, will enable you to undertake those tasks fruitfully while also enabling you to remain yourself.

In an age of anxiety it should not surprise us if the church reflects anxiety.

In an age that privileges quantifiable success it should not surprise us if the church gets caught up in measuring outcomes.

In an age that celebrates celebrity it should not surprise us if the church wants to be noticed.

But you and I are simply called to be faithful in the one thing given to us. To be priests. The rest will be sorted, but all in good time. And goodness always comes from God.

After all, you have Christ in you, the hope of glory.

If we give our simple 'Yes' to God, if we offer our faith ('green as a leaf', as R. S. Thomas says of the kingdom), then we will discover that grace fills our lives and we can both fulfil this calling with joy and perhaps, most important of all, remember who we really are.

As Kingfishers Catch Fire

As kingfishers catch fire, dragonflies draw flame;
As tumbled over rim in roundy wells
Stones ring; like each tucked string tells, each hung bell's
Bow swung finds tongue to fling out broad its name;
Each mortal thing does one thing and the same:
Deals out that being indoors each one dwells;
Selves – goes itself; myself it speaks and spells,
Crying *What I do is me: for that I came.*

I say more: the just man justices;
Keeps grace: that keeps all his goings graces;
Acts in God's eye what in God's eye he is –
Christ – for Christ plays in ten thousand places,
Lovely in limbs, and lovely in eyes not his
To the Father through the features of men's faces.

Gerard Manley Hopkins
1844–99

The Priest

The priest picks his way
Through the parish. Eyes watch him
From windows, from the farms;
Hearts wanting him to come near.
The flesh rejects him.

Women, pouring from the black kettle,
Stir up the whirling tea-grounds
Of their thoughts; offer him a dark
Filling in their smiling sandwich.

Priests have a long way to go,
The people wait for them to come
To them over the broken glass
Of their vows, making them pay
With their sweat's coinage for their correction.

He goes up a green lane
Through growing birches; lambs cushion
His vision, He comes slowly down
In the dark, feeling the cross warp
In his hands; hanging on it his thought's icicles.

'Crippled soul', do you say? looking at him
From the mind's height; 'limping through life
On his prayers. There are other people
In the world, sitting at table
Contented, though the broken body
And the shed blood are not on the menu.'

'Let it be so,' I say. 'Amen and amen.'

R. S. Thomas
1913–2000

Prayer

Prayer the Churches banquet, Angels age,
    Gods breath in man returning to his birth,
    The soul in paraphrase, heart in pilgrimage,
The Christian plummet sounding heav'n and earth;
Engine against th' Almightie, sinners' towre,
    Reversed thunder, Christ-side-piercing spear,
    The six-daies world-transposing in an houre,
A kinde of tune, which all things heare and fear;
Softnesse, and peace, and joy, and love, and blisse,
    Exalted Manna, gladnesse of the best,
    Heaven in ordinarie, man well drest,
The milkie way, the bird of Paradise,
    Church-bels beyond the starres heard, the souls bloud,
    The land of spices; something understood.

George Herbert
1593–1633

What I do is me: for this I came

1 Holiness, wisdom and mercy

God is not interested in our morality,
only our holiness,
which is something quite different.

God does not want clever priests
but wise ones
who understand
that mercy triumphs over judgement.

We will also be present
to accompany and encourage
to learn and to teach
to listen and listen
– a listening that is not waiting
for an opportunity to speak.

We keep alive the rumour of God,
declaring that God takes flesh
and walks alongside us, in us.

We can often be the toastmasters –
sometimes the party pooper
delivering the bad news
that not everything is OK.

2 Stuck in the middle

Who is the priest in this Anglican tradition?

She is not a preacher
– although she will preach.

She is not an evangelist
– although she will share Good News.

She is not a pastor
– although she exercises loving pastoral care.

She is not a teacher
– although teaching will be second nature.

She is not a Mass machine
– although celebrating the sacraments
will be of the essence,
at the very heart, of her priesthood.

She is a human being who is learning to get in the way,
not as a barrier but as a stepping stone
and like all stones a bit scuffed and worn.

She will be someone content to be stuck in the middle.

3 The scandal of the particular

We start from here: creation restored to its Creator.

Our priesthood is within the whole,
which is why it gets in the way.
It is both the same and different
to the call of every person,
all people, indeed the whole of creation.[1]

We are not set aside,
that is not the meaning of ordination.

On the contrary
we have been set in the middle
– such is the scandal of the particular.

We have not simply responded to a voice,
we have been given a voice.

A scandal is a stone to trip over,
and people will and they will curse.
But we can also be living stones
on which people can sit for a moment
to catch their breath.

---

1 'Christ in his love unites created reality with uncreated reality – How wonderful is God's loving kindness towards us! – and he shows that through grace the two are become one. The whole world enters wholly into the whole of God and by becoming all that God is, except identity of nature, it receives in place of itself the whole of God.' Maximos the Confessor (580–662), *Ambigua*.

4 Doing into being

Priests learn by doing ministry,
only then can they learn to *be* anything.

We live our way into a new way of thinking
just as infants do.

We cannot think our way into a new way of doing.

We learn to be priests only after ordination.
Our theological formation is just that,
the very necessary theological formation.
It doesn't make us priests.

That requires the grace of ordination
which is real and persistent.
This should be a comfort
to all ordinands who feel inadequate.
You are! We all are.

This is part of our sanctification.
It starts, as with all new languages,
conjugating the verb 'to be'.
We discover that 'I am' is not about us,
but about God, who *is* I am.

The conjugation
is the doing that provides the being.

God is the ground of our being,
who teaches us to be
through the conjugation of holiness.

5 Love and the image of God

Love is the something that defines us as human
and our joy in being *imago Dei* – the image of God.

We may often be *homo faber*: humanity the maker.
We are rarely *homo sapiens*: humanity the wise.

But we are made to be *homo caris*: humanity the lover,
indeed perhaps even *homo eros* and *homo agape*:
humanity the knower of the consummation of God's love.

Yet our age
has so individualized faith and love,
that what should be a covenant between persons

so often becomes simply a contract between individuals.

6 This-ness

When most human beings lived in small worlds,
rarely travelling more than a few miles from home,
maybe they naturally had a better understanding
of 'this-ness'[2] than those of us who live such mobile lives.

But this is unlikely.
Deep in every person there is a restlessness
which makes us look beyond the here and now
and long for something else,
something different, something new.

We may not know it,
but this is our longing for God,
our longing to go home.
Every person has this, somewhere,
even though it may have been buried
under life's detritus.

It distracts us from attending to the here and now.

For God is not elsewhere
but closer to us than we are to ourselves.

We are always home, but we cannot believe it.
This is the finest deceit, one of sin's great achievements.
Priests must learn to attend to the 'this-ness' of things.

---

2 The mystical theology term for 'this-ness' is *haecceity.*

7 *Hiraeth*, lament and joy: hope

The Welsh word *hiraeth*
is not easily translated.

'Longing' or 'homesickness'
are too simple for it also holds a sense of grief.

It is not nostalgia but a sensing of deep connection, of loss,
with the curious hope that all is not lost in God.

Loss is placed into the hands of God's loving kindness
and this enables us to lament.
Lament is the foundation of joy.
Lament is not sorrow, but beyond sorrow,
holding grief and hope.

Hiraeth describes the experience of lament.

Beyond loss and longing comes joy, though joy with tears.[3]

Priests learn *hiraeth* so that lamenting with joy
they witness to hope,
the sure and certain hope of resurrection.

Hiraeth makes us long to go home.

And our home is God,
who longs to welcome us to the present moment.

---

3 'Joy with tears', Diadochus of Photike, fifth century CE.

8 Discipleship

Discipleship is holiness in evolution,
remembering who we are and where we came from
and all that wisdom
spilling out in love of and service to all and everything.

Being the love of God
so that people can be themselves
and creation celebrated.

There is a great deal of doing,
but it is mostly the doing of simply being there,
attending to the moment and its needs,
manifested in the joys and wounds of our neighbour.

Discipleship is not a programme of events
nor about making others like us,
but more like themselves:
the image of God,
the body of Christ.

Remembering who we are,
the outworking of baptism, communion, grace.

The shock of not needing to be right.

9 Mercy triumphs over judgement[4]

Justice, judgement, judging.

This triad is a key pathology of our age.
Justice, judgement, judging are blind.
And so they should be.
They attempt to make everyone equal and fail.

Mercy is wide eyed
longing to recognize each person as precious.
Mercy is halfway to succeeding
simply by wanting to.

Justice, judgement and judging are forbidden by Jesus.

In this way mercy triumphs over judgement.

Priests must choose
mercy over justice.

Judgement and judging we leave to God.

Mercy God shares with us.

---

4 James 2.13.

10 No longer ego

> I have been crucified with Christ;
>   and it is no longer I[5] who live,
> but it is Christ who lives in me.
> *Galatians 2.19b–20*

This is ascesis: spiritual exercise, combat,
the deliberate engagement with the hard work
of taking up our cross and following Jesus.

The real enemy is us. We do battle with ourselves.
The battle is not to do or achieve
but simply to learn to let go,
to stop wanting power and control which is sin's root.
In our raw and unsanctified state
we all want power and control
over ourselves, over others, over nature – and God.

The battle is not to be rid of our ego
but to let the ego retire into the background
still there to motivate us when we need it
but no longer able to make us
turn everything into a story about ourselves.

Thus we shall begin to learn apatheia
which is not carelessness
but a positive indifference,
the interior freedom
by which we can enjoy without owning
and lose without resentment.
This is not a cold disinterest
but a faithful joy that all things are safe in God.

---

5 In Greek: 'it is no longer *ego* who lives …'

11 Humility and humiliation

Humbleness and humility
are most certainly not the same thing.
Anyone can present themselves as humble
but humility is a different game.

The kingdom of God
is not available to the outwardly humble.

The kingdom is, however,
the place where we learn humility.

Humility can only be learnt by being humiliated.[6]

We need a regular, indeed daily, dose of humiliation
so that we learn to accept it without rancour.

This kind of humiliation
is not allowing ourselves to be abused,
which is always evil and must be resisted,
but those moments when our own foolishness
lights up the room.

We must welcome those moments,
as James tells us, as friends and with joy.[7]
These are painful but necessary.
Humiliation is the groundwork of ascesis.[8]

---

6 Richard Rohr OFM: 'Pray for one good humiliation every day.'
7 James 1.2.
8 'Ascesis has no value if it does not help to deepen humility.' Oliver Clément,
The Roots of Christian Mysticism, Welwyn Garden City: New City, 2017,
p. 281.

12 Holiness

Jesus wasn't crucified for being a paragon of morality.
He was crucified for being holy.

Morality is what humans invent
to cover up our alienation from each other,
from our environment, from God.
We blackmail ourselves
into behaving in socially acceptable ways.

It turns out, however,
that we all gladly join in the deception
because we cannot resist the challenge
of showing how good we are,
either for real (as if!) or by subterfuge.

Holiness can then be deferred.
Holiness is then for special people,
saints, great individuals, preferably dead ones.

For Christ plays in ten thousand places

13 The kingdom is not

The kingdom is not when we've got it right:
the kingdom is falling down a hole.

The kingdom is not when we've fed everyone:
it's seeing the view, flat on our backs, for the first time.

The kingdom is not when we finally get it organized:
it's when we stand on the rake
and the handle swings up and cracks us on the nose,
such is the bizarreness of the kingdom.

The kingdom is not when we've set the prisoners free:
it's when we realize we are the prisoners, and we're free
    to go.

The kingdom is not the beginning, the middle or the end:
it's centred everywhere and bounded nowhere.

The kingdom is not justice:
the kingdom is righteousness which is something
    else entirely:
the liberation of mercy triumphing over judgement.

The kingdom is not achieving:
the kingdom is peace which is pregnant space.

The kingdom is not travelling hopefully
(which is mere optimism, that parody of hope):
the kingdom is joy in the Holy Spirit in the coldest wind.

> For the kingdom of God is not food and drink
> but righteousness and peace and joy in the Holy Spirit.
> *Romans 14.17*

14 Godly wisdom

Godly wisdom
is a gift that reveals that the kingdom of God has
   come near.
It is both free and costs us everything.
Godly wisdom is jostled in the marketplace.
This marketplace is Isaiah's public square[9]
where truth stumbles in the noise of commerce and debate.

How to walk through that
and keep oneself unstained by the world
as James charged us to do?[10]

Wisdom, it is said, is skilful living.
Skill, art, craft and connoisseurship
are the personal outworking
of the virtues of the kingdom.
They are far more important
than information can ever be.

Priests are not in the business of being right,
or convincing others to think like us,
but in negotiating the stream of life
in a way that is helpful to those in the stream around us.

---

9 Isaiah 59.14.
10 James 1.27.

15 Patience

Biding God's time requires patience.
The trouble with patience is that you have to wait for it.
The unbridled ego is always impatient
and gorges itself on the love of self
which is the contradiction of beauty.
This is *philautia*, the love of self
or rather, the disordered love of self.

Self-love causes
our forgetfulness – God, who is God?
our dullness – our neighbour is not our concern
our ignorance – the loss of the capacity to wonder.

Spiritual exercise, ascesis, means waking up
from the sleepwalk of life.[11]

God is beautiful.
The unbridled ego makes us unable to appreciate it,
and we are asleep to true beauty.

Sin is blind to beauty.

Learning patience, bridling the ego,
means waking up and being self-aware enough
to accept that if we don't have what we desire, it's OK
and that change will come at its speed not ours.

Patience means biding – that is abiding – in God's time.
It allows us to appreciate the beauty of God
and to enjoy the 'this-ness' of things.

---

11 Oliver Clément, *The Roots of Christian Mysticism*, Welwyn Garden City:
New City, 2017, p. 130.

16 The body and its weight

We can no more build the kingdom
than we can paint the solar system.

The church and kingdom are equal partners
in the divine economy.

They are
the musical score and the sound from the instrument.

They are
the script and its acting out.

But don't try working out which is which.

The kingdom is the mass of the body of Christ –
the true Christ, that is, the heart of creation.

17 Virtually valueless

The kingdom of God
Is not a place of moral or political aspirations.

It has no values.

Only the theological virtues of faith, hope and love.

It does not worry about power and control.

This is why it's the wildest place to live
and safest place to be.

18 The power of keys

Priests can do great good or great harm.[12]

Forgiveness,
and the withholding of forgiveness,
is the only power in the kingdom.

Priests can liberate or incarcerate others.
This binding and loosing is a burden we can only carry
by prayer and grace.

The power of keys, both binding and loosing,
is always the power to set free,
and if freedom does not follow
it is abuse,
which is the priesthood of Caiaphas
who used his position for power and control over others,
which is the root of all abuse.

---

12 Melissa, my wife, told me this.

19 Prayer

While we are learning to live lightly
we can learn to resonate with
the 'unforced rhythms of grace',[13]
which see us through the dark,
even though the pain may be immense.

Yet so much prayer is really about me,
and my experience of God,
instead of God's experience of me,
and then the dark can terrify.

Prayer is
the kingdom turning from day to night and to day again.

The kingdom is recognizing that in curved space
sunset and sunrise are actually the same,
for as the sun goes down here
it rises there.

---

13 Matthew 5, from Eugene H. Peterson, *The Message: The Bible in Contemporary Language*, Carol Stream, IL: NavPress, 2002.

20 The end of all things is at hand

Worship is more about gazing than praising.
And that gazing, that action of inaction,
starts with God gazing at us,
like a newborn's mother
lost in adoration of this small person on her breast.

The important thing is to turn up.

The Eucharist solemnly proclaims ...
look at, listen to, smell, sense, feel,
take and eat the bread, take and drink the wine.
Smell, feel, sense, apprehend,
but let us not think that we know.

There are words, but they are just back-up,
a commentary on the action, an invitation
to the doing of nothing.

The kingdom of God is a party
where the best wine is kept until last
and yet it is always being served
because now is the very end
because now is the day of salvation.[14]

---

14 2 Corinthians 6.2.

21 'If you wish, you can be all flame'[15]

Worship is not something we do.
Worship is done to us.
Worship is something into which we are drawn
like moths to the consuming flame.

Like Moses' burning bush
we are not consumed but sanctified.

Our God is a consuming fire.[16]

Priests are called to be burned out in holiness
– losing ourselves in finding ourselves in God.
That's the only employment available in the kingdom.

Holiness is our participation in God,
our divinization, *theosis*.[17]

---

15 A saying of Abba Joseph, one of the Desert Fathers, in *The Joy of the Saints*,
ed. Robert Llewelyn, London: Darton, Longman and Todd, 1988, p. 104.
16 Hebrews 12.29.
17 *Theosis* is the term used in the Eastern Church, meaning *divinization*. In
mystical theology it is a key concept in growing in holiness. It is the outworking of being *in Christ* (St Paul), *one* with God (Julian of Norwich) or, as the
Elizabethan Anglican Divine Richard Hooker called it, *participation* in God.
It is both a state and a journey towards a state.

22 Anamnesis

Anamnesis is a different quality of remembering
and it takes time to remember,
at least *this* kind of remembering takes time,
for it brings past and future into the now and
makes it manifest, puts it back together
re-membered.

The content of this remembering is not facts
but truth as love
rather than truth as right thinking

Orthodoxy is also *orthodoxa* – 'right glory' –
truth is more about right glory, right joy, right loving
than right thinking.

The kingdom is glory, joy, love, in the Holy Spirit.

What else would the Holy Spirit,
the 'Lord, the giver of life' be about?
And so to be reminded is in fact to be re-minded.

Then, our minds are not simply renewed,
we learn to think beyond our minds,
which is what *metanoia*,[18] repentance, means.

The kingdom is remembering things
we never knew we knew.
For Christ plays in ten thousand places.

---

18 *Meta* – beyond, *nuos* – mind.

23 Remembering who we are

We receive our Christian name in baptism.
It may have been our name before
but when it is used under the threefold water
it is a new name.

We may know our name,
but who we are, whose we are, where we come from –
these we will have forgotten
by the time we are four or five years old,
and often much sooner.

Baptism is the sacrament and celebration
that marks the start of our journey
of remembering who we are.

It is our priestly privilege and duty
to liberally spread abroad baptismal grace.

Baptismal grace is prevenient – it goes ahead of us.
It is actual grace – it returns to God all that it touches.
It is habitual grace – we live inside it as it lives inside us.

Graciously growing in holiness is identical
to remembering who we are.

The kingdom is the celebration of our identity.

This party is always going on
but we are too often
undressed in our concerns
to be let in.

24 The great thanksgiving

The Eucharist takes us back to the future
and the heavenly banquet
in which the hoi polloi are guests
the very same hoi polloi refused re-entry
when Eve and Adam spoiled the gentle party
that was Eden.

The Eucharist is a continual mercy
until it becomes continuous mercy,
the eternal joy of which we can catch a taste, a smell.

It is the thankfulness of owing everything
but knowing we have nothing to pay.

The kingdom is where we are
when we learn to have this joy.

Lovely in limbs, and lovely in eyes not his

25 The church does not have a mission

Mission is never just mission.

It is,
commission: beginning things together
transmission: passing faith, hope and love
intermission: space is essential
admission: letting others in
submission: serving
remission: forgiving
emission: because there's always rubbish
photoemission: light for the world
pretermission: knowing what to leave
decommission: celebrating death
intromission: the journey inwards
manumission: setting free
dismission: especially in peace
permission: for each to be themselves

but never, never, ever just 'mission'.

26 When our bodies lie in the dust

The sacrament of baptism is the promise
that God knows who we are
even though we have forgotten.

We are ensouled bodies not embodied souls.
The difference is, literally, crucial.
It allows us to carry our cross.

The body after death is still the person
– that's why, despite the blasé Neoplatonism of modernity,
where ideas and the material coexists in a dualistic split,
we treat the body with deep respect.

Funerals are signs
of the kingdom being near
and the redemption of matter.

27 Speaking

Priests speak.
Vocation means not simply being called
but being given a voice.

Priests speak with others – which really means listening.

Priests speak to – to situations rather than to individuals,
for that would simply be judging them.

Priests speak for those who are unable to speak for themselves
because of grief, disability, poverty, class, race,
or some other marginalizing, silencing, situation.

We will speak for a family at a funeral
as together we pay tribute to their loved one.

We will speak for a family or individual
who cannot get heard in the surgery, the council,
the school or the court.

We will speak for the person
who is not being listened to
by some other person or group.

We must do this without them losing their dignity.

That unhearing group may, sometimes, be the church.

28 Pzazz

King David leaped before the Lord with pzazz.[19]

As ministers before the Lord
priests learn to lead God's people in worship
not as managers or controllers
but as those who rejoice before the Most High,
alight with delight
that we have been privileged
and called to this great joy
of calling on God's people
to lift up their hearts in a shared drama,
a movement and a dance of praise and worship.

Worship is the celebration of the worth-ship of God
and it is a joy without limits
– a joy in and of the Holy Spirit
not an emotional self-expression.

This is what Michal failed to see in King David.[20]

---

19 2 Samuel 6.16.
20 2 Samuel 6.20–23.

29 'Tell all the truth, but tell it slant'[21]

How can the Teller of Tales
about a God being like an unjust judge,
or a landowner who pays everyone the same
no matter how long they've worked,
or a weak father
who gives his younger son his inheritance
without the slightest argument,
be telling the truth other than slant?

What about the man
who diddled the landowner out of the treasure
buried in his field
by simply forgetting to mention he'd found it
… and anyway what was he doing
rooting around in that field in the first place?

The kingdom of God is clearly for dodgy folk
for whom the truth is never quite what it seems.

And when asked a straight question
Jesus so rarely gave a straight answer.

---

21 Emily Dickinson, 'Tell all the truth but tell it slant', *The Poems of Emily Dickinson: Reading Edition*, Cambridge, MA: The Belknap Press of Harvard University Press, 1998.

30 Beware of the dogs, the cutters[22]

I think because I move,
I am an animated body
that has learned to speak.

But I am not my ideas.
I need not live in the fear we call rational doubt.

We act out of faith first, otherwise, like Piglet,
I would hide in bed all day with a headache.

Priests must be on guard against the Cartesian mistake:
'I think therefore I am.'
Doubtless, Descartes meant well by doubting.
But to doubt everything but oneself is insanity.

But what Descartes taught turned out to be unbelief –
a refusal to go beyond the perceived self.
This is a disaster, but who can see it?

Anglican priesthood has its roots
in that liminal space between the Middle Ages
and our age which we call Modernity
an age of doubt and anxiety
which may well be entering its last decades.

Beware of the dogs, the cutters
who doubt everything that is not their opinion.
They think they are their ideas.
But they are not.

---

22 Philippians 3.2.

31 Union

We were made by God,
we have never been lost to God,
though God appeared lost to us,
and growing our souls
is the out-working of baptismal grace
which reminds us who we are.

As union with God has its effect we see more clearly
that we, with all the saints, are the image of God
and grow in God's likeness –
that is, in holiness and love.

This is the Pauline idea of sanctification
and the grace of God,
the life of the Holy Spirit in us.
Being in Christ.

32 Wrath

> It is a fearful thing to fall into the hands of the living God.
> *Hebrews 10.31*

God's fearful love.
Such ambiguity.
God's love is a fire that burns without consuming,
like the burning bush.
But it also eradicates evil.

Our love for God
is at best a feeble reflection of that love,
and it is awe-filled and deeply astonished
that we should receive that which we reflect
in our created nature.

Wrath has nothing to do with an angry God
wanting to punish us.

Human wrath is about anger and violent vengeance.
God's vengeance is the outworking of divine love.

33 From glory to glory

Divinization, grace and glory.
These are the things that we are about.
We participate in Christ,
we are divinized by God's grace.

This is gift, grace,
and we may respond virtuously, but never morally.

We reflect God, for we are *imago Dei*,
and this is glorious.

If we dwell in this then we will live out of what we are,
or rather, what God is,
so that our doing may be holy.

34 Stewards of the mysteries of God

At times stewardship is about the management of things,
but as in managing a home and a family,
not a business.

At times stewardship is the work of guardianship,
not in the military sense,
but in the sense of being *in loco parentis*.
And like all good parents
our job is to help God's children
become grown up and independent,
not to keep them infantile and dependent.

At times stewardship is about being
toastmistresses and toastmasters
at the foretaste of the heavenly banquet
prepared for all peoples
we call the Eucharist.

35 No longer ego

Jesus calls us to take up our cross and follow him
... to lose our ego,
because ego has been crucified with Christ
... while assuring us that this won't be more than
    we can bear.

But of course, at times, it seems more than we can bear.

We can learn to resonate
with the 'unforced rhythms of grace',[23]
which see us through the darkness,
even though the pain may be immense.

But, and here's the thing:
The dark night of the soul is not always about pain.
Indeed as we pursue God
we shall enter the dark night without fear or pain,
because it will not be our darkness,
but in the holy dark we shall know God.

It will not be about us at all.

It is no longer ego who lives but Christ who lives in me.

---

23 Luke 11.28–30, from Eugene H. Peterson, *The Message: The Bible in Contemporary Language*, Carol Stream, IL: NavPress, 2002.

36 The last laugh

Despite the apparent injunction in Ephesians,
'Entirely out of place is obscene, silly, and vulgar talk',[24]
fun, humour and laughter are not outlawed –
although these have been seriously lacking
in the 2,000 years of church history
following the earth-walking of the Divine Comedian.

The first sign that Jesus gave in John's Gospel
was by providing copious gallons of the best wine
for a poor wedding breakfast in Cana.
If you can't see divine humour in this,
then what can you see?

We laugh with, never at.
True laughter always includes.

---

24 Ephesians 5.4.

For thine is the kingdom, power and the glory

37 Power and control

Priesthood is subversive
because all ministry in Christ is subversive.
Jesus lived and died a subversive.
He lived at odds with power and control.
Human society is simply turned on one principle:
power and control.
Power and control are the motivators of social intercourse
and the means for its apparent successes and
    inevitable failures.

Priestly subversion is not about power and control
but setting others free from it
because we know something of that freedom ourselves.

Those who are in Christ have no power
but the power of love
and no control
except the potential for the control of the self.

To live outside the structures of power and control –
that is, in but not of the world –
is to live freely in grace.

To engage with the world is a hazardous business
which we cannot avoid
and it demands that we hold to our subversion
and never become part of that in which we are set.

We must be things that are not.

38 The God delusion

God is a delusion that our minds conjure up
to make us think we are religious,
or people of faith,
or growing in discipleship,
or moral, or holy, or saved.

These thoughts about God are delusions.
We cannot think about God,
we can only manipulate our imagination
and pretend we are thinking about God.

Can we imagine love?
We can only imagine what love does
but love itself is beyond us
for God is love
and like David's arrows[25]
God is beyond us
and we must flee from the Saul in our minds
who would pin our delusion to the wall
as though God were a butterfly in a collection.

Yet we easily persist in our mental constructs
as though we had some idea about God,
some notion that we are in the know
when all that is required is to be empty,
a space for the Holy Spirit to fill,
to look beyond where the arrows fell
and the freedom of the cave of Adullam.[26]

25 1 Samuel 20.22.
26 1 Samuel 22.1.

39 Things to come

People have always wanted to know the future.
Fortune-telling of one sort or another
goes all the way back to the earliest humans.
It is a sign both of increasing intelligence
and our complete lostness as a race
disorientated in our own environment as brains grew
and imagination began to fear tomorrow
and the availability of the next meal
a warm dry shelter
and the savagery of our neighbours.

When Christians worry about the future
– those things that are beyond a rational responsibility –
we have lost sight of being called to this, not that
of being called to here, not there
of being called to now, not then.

Today, not tomorrow, is the day of salvation.

Now abide: faith, hope and love, these three

40 Faith, hope and love

Faith and hope are the length and breadth of love.
Love is its own depth.
That is why it's the greatest of the three.

41 Faith is love asserting itself

Faith is love asserting itself.
To have faith is simply to know we are loved.
No more, no less.
Faith, in this way,
is the place where the rubber of love hits the road of life.
Once we know we are loved then we know that all things,
all things,
are loved eternally.

To have faith is not to exercise some confident act of will
but, in simplicity, to allow oneself to be carried along
by the current of grace in the stream of love
till we are finally emptied out in the sea of God's eternity.

42 Hope is love seeing beyond the inevitable death of all things

Hope is love seeing beyond the inevitable death of
all things.

Hope is love asserting that it is not only Lord of life,
but Lord of death too.

Hope is the quiet assurance
the overshadowing
of seeing the power of resurrection through the pain
of death.

Because resurrection is the inevitable outcome of love.

43 Love is not an emotion

Love is not feelings or the shifting chemicals in our brains,
nor the surge of electric connections.
Love is the non-thing
above, beyond, below, behind all things,
the ground of our being,
the very Godliness of God.

We love because we were first loved.

44 This triad is not a linear progression

Faith, hope and love, these three
are not the corners of the baseball pitch:
we do not score by running around them.
They are a reflection of the Holy Trinity
who brought them into being.

They mutually indwell each other
but like the human Christ,
faith and hope are less than love
because they are love's incarnation.

The trick is not to do arithmetic
as three doesn't mean three in this language
– there is no counting in the Trinity –
and no numerical dependency
in the interplay of the one and the three.

Faith can only be seen in the corner of our eyes.
Look at faith, and it's gone.
Look at the task of love that needs doing
and faith is clearly there
in our peripheral vision.

Hope is even more elusive of our gaze.
It is the long shadow of love
coming from over our shoulder
assuring us that we are in the umbra of love's care.
We cannot turn to see its origin.
Because hope comes from God's future.
And we aren't there yet.

Faith, hope and love, these three:
the threefold unity that cannot be grasped
by the tools of quantitative analysis.

45 Let hope keep you joyful

To stand in the shadow of hope
is not to whistle in the dark,
but to feel the protection
of love's hand.

Cheap hope is common enough:
it'll be all right (maybe)
we can get through this (maybe not)
I've got this (really?)
we can do this together (possibly).

There is no cheap hope for the drowned child
the incinerated
the bombed
the parched
the empty

for they are dead.

Worldly hope is for the living.
This hope is for those who know death
    precedes resurrection
and the renewal of all things
which is the hope that keeps us joyful
even when pessimism is the only realistic option.

Hope is the valley of the shadow.

46 Faith is knowing we are loved[27]

This is the core, the livid spine
the jangling nerve cortex of the gospel.
Knowing we are loved.

Yet so many versions of faith evade this
manipulate this, control this
in order to keep the faithful asking for more.

So many people travel through life
for years and years
never really believing
– truly knowing –
that they are loved.

But if the penny drops
everything changes
and the ranters
the shouters
the managers
and the statisticians
the claimers of charisms

become to us what they are –
a freak show in the religious circus
deserving our mercy
our love

because now we can, in fact, love them
because we know we are loved.

---

27 'Faith is knowing we are loved. It is answer love with love.' Oliver Clément,
The Roots of Christian Mysticism, Welwyn Garden City: New City, 1998.

Joyful, simple and merciful, according to the gospel

47 Joyful

To be joyful is to receive a gift that arrives
like a pass-the-parcel prize.

It needs unwrapping in the gaze of life
while the music is momentarily paused.

It is joy in the midst of all the stress and strain, the sad and
    the bad.

Joy refuses to go away
because joy knows that it has nothing to do with feelings
or ideas of happiness

though it might pal up with contentment
even when no one else can see
what there's to be content about.

48 Simple

Simplicity requires oneness
and oneness requires an undefended self.
From infancy we have learned to defend our body,
   our emotions
our space and our dignity
and so re-live the tragedy of Eve and Adam
embarrassed by their fig-leaf-demanding nakedness.

Simplicity requires a clear understanding
of what matters
and an ability, like Occam's razor
to cut out all that is not essential
all the fat, the verbiage, the distractions
to be at one, uncomplicated by the many.

49 Merciful

Mercy is the final triumph
the actuality of love
having the last word.

Until we are 'surprised by joy'
and learn the simplicity of being undefended
we will deny mercy its triumphal march
through the backstreets of life.

Mercy has no place in the public square.
For truth always stumbles in the public square
and Tiananmen is an icon of what humans do[28]
when they build their towers and plazas
their monuments and arches.
They remind truth that it wasn't invited.

In the backstreets, the alleys and the wasteland
there is hope.

Wisdom cries on the High Street
but her words die on the breeze.

Mercy walks quietly through the backyards
touching the hoi polloi,
who alone might benefit from her injustice.

---

28 Tiananmen Square in Beijing was the place of a massacre of student
demonstrators by the Chinese army in 1989.

This, here, now

50 This, here, now

This, here, now abide these three
and the greatest of these is now
because now is where here is
and here is where this is.

Time comes from behind us
over our shoulder
and we see the future dimly, in a burnished mirror
we go backward to the future.
We see where we have been
and celebrate the faithfulness of God
to whom we leave the future also.

In the Eucharist we celebrate
a foretaste of the heavenly banquet
the future now.

There is only
this
here
now.

The anatomy of apathy

51 Heart

Apathy, *apatheia*, in the life of the soul, is the centre
of activity.

The heart of apathy is living without passion
requiring the deepest commitment
without which we will simply be playing a heartless game
of religion.

Apathy is the state of the soul that has learned to let go of
all passion
so that it can discover what it means
to be truly alive in and to the present moment
without the present moment having any purchase on her
or any entitlement to ownership or loyalty.

For the only purchase the soul has is that for the Holy Dove
to rest
and the only ownership is that of her Creator,
who doesn't think in terms of owning, but Oneing.[29]

---

29 See note 15 on p. 22.

This covenant is the heart of apathy
that which pumps the lifeblood of grace
through the arteries and veins of who we are before God.
A covenant which itself is a gift of grace.

The heart of apathy is the apathy of the heart.

52 Breath

To learn to allow life to unfold in front of us, drawing us in
fulfilling our daunting obligation
but never concerning ourselves with outcomes
such as success or failure.

Only the one outcome of love concerns us
which is, of course, that daunting obligation:
the final demand on us in this life.

To be apathetic is far from not caring, or being laid back.
It is actively being still and positively doing nothing.
No wonder it demands everything of us.
It is the life of godly quietness.

While this godly quietness
is about peace in the world
it turns out that such a peace cannot exist
unless it is the expression of the indwelling of
    godly quietness
which is only truly at home with our apathy.

Thus our breathing
that is the rhythm of drawing in and out the holy *ruach*
    of God
– or perhaps better being breathed in and out by God –
is the only source of godly quietness
and this gives oxygen to the soul.

This is deep prayer, costing not less than everything.

53 Blood

> There is a river whose streams make glad the city of God.
> *Psalm 46.4*, Common Worship

Joy and gladness are the effects of apathy.

Joy is beyond happiness as the sun is beyond the earth.

Joy is the insistence that love was right all along, and all
shall be well.

Joy is the infusion of actual grace when things hurt
the most.

Joy is the lifeblood of apathy.

The marks of a
Jesus-shaped mission

54 The cross

The cross is the only thing we have, it sends us,
it is what we carry, it is what we leave behind.
For the cross cannot fail but to carry the resurrection.

The cross is the first, perhaps the only, mark of mission.

55 The Christ child

The long job of mission is incarnation.

It starts with the Annunciation
nine months gestation
a birth
a childhood (shaped by the life of a refugee)
an adolescence (shaped by exploring boundaries)
a young adulthood (shaped by silently getting on with the
    job in hand).

It is about a ratio of 11:1
11 years of silence and waiting
for every year of speaking and acting.

It is a patience,
a patience that is willing to wait out the chronological time
in order to prioritize the right time.

56 The man Christ Jesus

Mission
is about
making friends
touching untouchables
healing the sick
telling outrageous stories
rebuking the religious
and mostly ignoring the powerful.

It is about keeping company with
all sorts, posh and poor,
men and women,
children and the aged.

It's also about telling it like it is
and raising the dead.

The problem with resurrection of course
is that first there has to be a death.

57 Cock crow

Peter's ego
rocking back and forth between indignation
and over self confidence
was humiliated.

From then on
Peter learned that he wasn't who he thought he was
but was closer to Jesus than (almost) anyone.

A church that is built on this rocky truth
propped against the cornerstone which is Christ
must also learn humiliation
as the cock crows
and we know we have denied our Lord three times.

When we denied that children were abused
when we privileged men over women
when we excluded the different, the disabled, the elderly
we denied him three times.

Until then mission is a busyness
designed to make us feel good about ourselves.

But if we hear the cock crow we can weep
and our tears will help us see clearly
and our service of people will be sharper, quieter
done in humility and grace.

Our mission will have begun.

58 The purple robe

Power and control
are the twins from hell that bedevil the church
with their insatiable demands.

The purple robe was uncut
kept whole in order to steal authority from the one
who truly had the right to carry it on his shoulders.

A church that manipulates its members
ties people into demands it cannot expect them to meet
holding power and control
in clergy
(or laity
– no matter, it's all the same)
is a church that has tossed the dice and thought it had
    won something.

Mission begins when the church empties itself
a kenotic surrender
a loss of power and control
a nakedness as others steal the purple robe
and we are seen
undefended.

A church
gives the purple robe away.

59 The nail-pierced hands and feet and the spear-pierced side

Prayer, says George Herbert,
is the 'Christ-side-piercing spear'.

What an extraordinary thing to say
but he who saw the water and blood
bore witness
simply by standing still and watching.

John teaches us prayer as he stands by the cross.
There are no words
for the prayer is our 'dart of longing love',
as the author of *The Cloud of Unknowing* says,
and it opens the side of Christ
and prayer is real.

Without this kind of prayer, mission is merely activism
and rushing around
demanding attention.

A diseased understanding of mission is the kind of thing
that can come out only by prayer.

Then the butchered hands are made visible to those
ready to see them.

60 The crown of thorns

Christ the King enthroned on the cross.
Majestas.[30]

The crown of thorns is the garland of resurrection
the guarantee
that death is not the end
but the necessary road to life.

Mission
is simply to be Mary Magdalen
reporting the risen Lord
to an incredulous audience
not clinging to Christ
but letting him go
so that he can cling to everyone.

This is the church in which we are to be priests.
This our mission
with nothing but a burial
in sure and certain hope
of resurrection.

> I have been crucified with Christ;
> and it is no longer I who live,
> but it is Christ who lives in me.
> And the life I now live in the flesh
> I live by faith in the Son of God,
> who loved me and gave himself for me.
> *Galatians* 2.20

---

30 *The Majestas* is the statue by the twentieth-century sculptor Sir Jacob Epstein KBE of Christ in Majesty on the *pulpitum* in Llandaff Cathedral. I was ordained priest underneath it in 1982.